# THE JOURNEY OF
# A CERTIFIED
# NURSE ASSISTANT

# THE JOURNEY OF A CERTIFIED NURSE ASSISTANT

## In Real Time
### WE HELP YOU RISE AND SHINE

## Barbara Ali

PALMETTO
PUBLISHING
Charleston, SC
www.PalmettoPublishing.com

*The Journey of a Certified Nurse Assistant*

Copyright © 2023 Barbara Ali

Print Book Edition 2023

The information contained in this book is intended for
informational purposes only and should not be construed as
legal advice on any subject matter. You should not act or refrain
from acting based on any content included in this book without
seeking legal or other professional advice. I have re-created events
from my memories of them. In order to maintain anonymity for
instances, names and places to protect individual's privacy.

Paperback ISBN: 979-8-218-95353-9

# Dedication

To my mother, who encouraged me to get a nursing career, she was way passed her senior years when she started working as a (PCA) patient care aide. My mother used to say to us be a nurse. She did share some of her experiences as a PCA. I sympathized with her and did not want her to do that type of work. She loved the type of work that she was doing but felt that it was too unnecessarily competitive. I am thankful to her for sharing because it got me through a lot of adversities in my new career. I eventually took her advice. I too had to deal with a lot of jealousy and competition. Some of us have heard the saying, what won't break you, will make you stronger. I feel good about my life as a certified nursing assistant. I dressed and carried myself in the best manner when it came to behavior and appearance. When My daughter finished high school, she too wanted to be a certified nursing assistant, so she thought. She received a certificate and worked one night with adult patients and decided it was not for me. It is a decision that the individual must make for themselves and sometimes experience can help us make those decisions. She is now a nurse because she too was encouraged by (my mother) her grandmother. She enjoys working in pediatrics.

# CONTENTS

# INTRODUCTION

I became a banker at an early age. I was a quiet child so bless the teacher who provided the necessary routes to take so that I could achieve that goal. I enjoyed my experience as a banker for many years. I did not get to travel to different countries, but I interacted with a lot of people from around the world via telex and telephone communication. Besides, there were so many diverse cultures from around the world in New York City, I did not think that I was missing out. I was skinny so I got fed by diverse cultures. I am thinking that they thought that I was hungry, nevertheless the food was delicious. As technology progressed and time passed, I began to feel like a robot. Traveling from Queens, New York to Manhattan, New York, Wall Street on the subway daily for years can also take a toll. The subway compartments on the train were usually jammed packed to capacity. I changed my career after moving to Virginia in the year 1991.

In the following pages I would like to share with you some of my experiences as a (CNA) certified nursing assistant and the reason I chose this path and how personally rewarding it has been through the years. It is rewarding because I met and helped a lot of people. When people in the medical field achieve their license and degrees, they are happy to acquire such an accomplishment. I have met many certified nursing assistants who felt belittled, so they became disgruntled and wanted to become a nurse. Some had a tough time achieving that goal. In no way am I trying to discredit anyone. I am saying to the certified nursing assistant, be happy to receive your certificate if this is the career that you choose and be the best that you can be. I attribute my concept of thinking on how to maneuver and conduct some of my most challenging task to the Honorable Elijah Muhammad.

# MY FIRST ASSIGNMENT

My first assignment, I prayed an earnest prayer to do something different from banking. I was not sure what I wanted to do; however, I knew that I did not want to do banking work anymore. My first assignment as a (PCA) patient care aide came without training in 1994. I wanted to work, and I wanted to do something different from my past career.

I walked around downtown Richmond and noticed an employment agency, so I went in to apply for a job. I filled out the necessary paperwork. I was hired on the same day. The interviewer told me that my assignment would be for a week as a live in. I agreed and the payment was for three hundred dollars to be paid at the end of the assignment week.

The assignment was in another county, so a friend drove me over because I did not know how to drive. I never learned while living in New York, besides, there was a bus on every corner, and they ran frequently. When I arrived at the house, I was greeted by a couple who referred to themselves as boyfriend and girlfriend. They introduced me to a big lady in a huge wheelchair. They told me that she liked eggs and cheese and hurriedly left. About ten minutes later her sister arrived and assured me that the assignment was only for a week. She stayed for about ten minutes then she left. When I sat down at the table across from her and we were staring at each other, reality sat in. I finally realized that I did not ask them any questions and they did not volunteer to share any information regarding her. I asked her "what would you like for lunch?" She replied, "they only give me cheese and eggs." I thought when we constantly consume cheese it makes us constipated. There was meat in the refrigerator, so I fixed her a sandwich and a cup of tea.

After giving her lunch and tidying up, I went to the bathroom. She was in a motorized wheelchair, so she rode over and pushed the bathroom door open. Her actions did not phase me and that is because I had other things on my mind such as her being three hundred and fifty pounds with (MS) multiple sclerosis. We just sat at the table, she was nodding and waking up abruptly. I gave her can soup, toast and can fruit for dinner, I made it as tasty as possible. After dinner, I called her nephew and his girlfriend because I needed help putting her into bed. He did give me a phone number to call. I never got an answer, and I called numerous times. I decided to put her to bed early because I had to figure out what to do in that type of situation. I prayed pleading for help because I did not know what to do. I told her that I was going to put her to bed. She did not reject it at all. She rolled her wheelchair next to the bed. I thought if I could align the wheelchair up with the bed that would help. I told her everything that I intended to do. I told her that I was not able to contact her family. She said, "my sister has cancer so she cannot help us." The wheelchair reclined back like a (cot) bed. I told her that I was going to roll her onto the bed. Mind you, she was three hundred and fifty pounds, and I was only one hundred and nineteen pounds. I pushed and noticed that there was no resistance on her part, so she rolled onto the bed. She was a mess. I thought, I am going to take my time. I told her that it was going to take a while to clean her up, she gently replied, "okay." I took about two hours to complete that task. Afterwards she asked me if I would sleep in a chair that was in her room. The chair was not a recliner. I then realized that she was afraid that I would leave. I firmly told her that I need to clean myself up. I kept affirming from the bathroom that I would be there shortly. The wheelchair was huge, so I was able to do the same with getting her back into the wheelchair the next morning. I took my time. I kid you not, I thought of myself, I am phenomenal. I knew then that the Great God was helping and protecting us.

I was able to manage such a demanding situation without the aid of others. Each day the assignment got easier. She shared with me that she was a high school teacher and a principal in the public school system. I took food out of the freezer to make meals for us. She was not hard to please when it came to her meals.

I came to like her and wanted to continue to help her, but I needed help. The end of the week had arrived, and no one came or contacted us. I called the agency to remind her that my week was up, I was not able to contact her family. She said to me, "so you are going to leave her too." I was confused for a moment because that had not crossed my mind. I called the number that they gave me and would not stop calling. I called every ten minutes until someone answered. Her nephew answered, so I proceeded to explain to him that I needed to get home in an emergency. He asked if I would be returning. I replied, "yes." The truth of the matter, prior to that I asked the patient to give me my check to sign so that when her sister came to visit, she could cash it for me. She did give me the check. I signed it and gave it back to her. I now realized that I would have to escape.

Within fifteen minutes the nephew and his girlfriend were there. I had already managed to get my check, so I left upon their arrival. I walked until the house was out of sight then I ran like I was being chased until I reached the bank. I signed in the three-hundred-dollar amount that was owned to me and got paid. I found my way back to Richmond. It took a while for me to make it back home to Richmond so by the time I got home, they had left so many messages demanding that I come back. They realized that I had gotten paid. I finally answered my phone, told them I was not coming back and if they did not like it, they could call the police. I never heard from them again.

I learned from that experience that some hard lessons are blessings. Try to keep peace and harmony while fixing some situations instead of cursing it. I patted myself on the back and realized what I wanted to do as a career.

*Note that many years after this assignment I came across the agency owner who asked if I was still working and that she wanted to work on an assignment. There were no ill feelings. She had gotten older and slower.

# CERTIFIED NURSING ASSISTANT

After working as a PCA for a few years, I was told that it was better to get certified as a nursing assistant. I became a nursing assistant in 1997. After getting certified, my pay was seven dollars and twenty-five cents. I knew that my worth would eventually be recognized. Being taught the proper handling of people helped me to be calm as I practiced my CNA skills. I got a position helping a man who was being hospitalized. A week after helping him, he asked me, "they don't pay you very much." I put a handle on that and said, "no sir." He spoke with his power attorney and paid me fifteen dollars an hour, even after that he paid me a generous salary. He also had a senior lady helping him who had been helping him for years. She began to tell him how they had grown old together and now they are both sick. I asked her not to speak to him as being old and sick if she plans to continue helping him. She resented me giving her that advice and began doing things that a sick ailing patient would do. I spoke with his power of attorney regarding her behavior. They advised that I not give her a tough time because she will have terrible things to say about me. I told them that I would not be cleaning up after her and will quit today. She stopped her disgusting behavior but continued to tell him about them being old and sick. They had planned to move him and have the senior lady work part time. He felt that she was feeling sick and tired, so he recommended part time work for her. The senior lady asked if I planned to work full time, I replied "yes." She quit because she wanted to work full time as before. She was well in her senior and retirement years so maybe she felt slighted. I would have collaborated peacefully with her as we did in the beginning. Two more CNAs were hired. When we work independently, sometimes we look at a job as being easy or laid back as one CNA said it. I always try to be watchful, observe the surroundings, making sure no slippery rugs are on the floors or furniture in the way. He used a walker and had a catheter inserted after his hospitalization. We do not close doors and relax as if we are home in our own bed. Sometimes the patient forgets that they have a catheter inserted or maybe because the door is closed you cannot hear the patient, so they attempt to care for themselves, as in his case a fall and the catheter pulled out causing hospitalization. I was with him until he was one hundred and three years old. He always referred to me as the little fellow. His family asked him, "why do you call her a little fellow, he replied because she's strong like one?" Those who met me knew that I was not a little fellow. What I learned from my first assignment, I carried into practice. I always treated him with respect and dignity. He would tell me stories about things that made me laugh, like the time his father went to New York to attend medical school. When he returned home, they thought that he was a big shot doctor riding that horse and buggy. I was told of how the man I helped, helped a lot of people. I listened to his videos as he explained his earlier life. I listened to his classical music and stories of what he did while being a teacher, judge, and navy sailor. One day he said to me, "we are a lot alike." We were not alike. He felt that way because I was able to help him live a peaceful life. Whenever I saw a sign of dementia or forgetfulness, I would ask him, "how old are you?" What I mean by that is, if he started talking about his mother as if she were alive. I would ask him, "how old are you?" He would reply, "my mother is dead, isn't she?" I would reply "yes." I enjoyed helping him and we both displayed generosity towards each other during his lifetime.

# BEING GOOD AT YOUR JOB OFTEN ATTRACTS MORE WORK

I was assigned to assist a lady who had paralysis on her right side. I was given some information and instructions. When I mentioned her stroke, one daughter felt that she did not have a stroke and the other one felt she did, but no one was direct with me. The daughter that said she did not have a stroke complained about the worthless CNAs. She also spoke about her mother in a manner that she thought that her mother did not understand. I asked her to be careful how she spoke about her mother because sometimes they understand what you are saying. The daughter replied, "she does not understand." When her daughter spoke, she would look from the daughter to myself as if she were waiting for me to respond. She found out shortly after that her mother in fact understood. Her mother was not able to speak anymore so she assumed that her mental state was totally lost. She had a bedside commode, so I pivoted her over from the bed, supporting her right side. She and her husband when I first started had her up and dressed when I arrived the first few times. When they realized how resourceful I was that changed. I had to manage her without their assistance. They would leave and return when it was time for me to leave. Things really did change because now they tried to treat her as if she had no paralysis. I looked around and found a food blender. I would make her food the consistency that she could swallow because she coughed a lot and coughed hard while eating. They made her breakfast in the morning. I was taught not to complain about the meals. What concerned me was her choking and aspiration while in my care. She enjoyed the meals that I made because I would try to feed her like I feed myself. The children would alternate between themselves with her care. The son told her that he was going to get her a hamburger and fries for lunch. She looked up at me with a stare. I said, "it's okay, if that's what you want for lunch." The son looked puzzled. He tried to keep a watch by tipping when he approached that day. I chopped that burger up in small chunks. You see, fluid would run from her eyes along with harsh coughing when she ate that coarse food. They were trying to keep her happy by feeding her what they thought she liked. I had my hands full. I continued to feed her the consistency and foods she enjoyed with me. I made nice cool salads and fruits included with her chicken meals. Her daughter said that she did not like salads but found out that she did like salads when prepared to her liking. Things were going well, but I also realized that once the daughter could see that she could understand what was being said, she was trying to coach her into getting me to do things that were unhealthy for her and myself. I am not a therapist. I told her daughter that she was beginning to fight with me to walk over to the chair instead of being helped with pivoting. I gave her mom superb support on the right side, so she did not realize how much I was supporting her. Her daughter was telling me how to walk her but was not showing me how it was done. One day a big mess was made because her mother was trying to care for herself, not realizing if I let her go, she would fall. I told her daughter and husband. The husband who did not smile when I first started was now smiling and said, "she has always had strong will power." I try to take all measures and precautions to prevent myself from getting hurt. I had previously hurt my rib muscle and used another technique until it healed. I was not going through that again. I called to let them know that I was not coming back. They had a week to prepare for someone else. They reached out asking if I could come back.

When CNAs are asked to do things that we are not qualified or trained to do we must think in terms of self-preservation whether it deems us worthless or not in the sight of someone else.

# SOMETIMES IT'S TIME TO CHANGE THAT DIET OR CONSISTENCY

I was sent to assist an elderly woman who was feeling poorly and was not eating. What we fail to realize sometimes is that these are people who have aged but still have some thought concept as to what they want and do not want. Sometimes we worry about them becoming too small or frail if they do not eat the foods that they have always eaten. They too can have a change of appetite. Sometimes they have enough sense to know who is interested in their wellbeing and who is not.

Sometimes they know that it is not intentional that we do not know, so they don't bother to try to explain it to us as to why they now have a change of appetite. Since it was okay for me to choose her meals, I added foods like fruits and vegetables with water content. I also gave her more water. She told me that she was constipated and yes, she was. She perked up and enjoyed her meals. As we age male or female we change inside and out. Some people realize the change, so we try to do what is necessary to keep us healthy. I have been in situations where people were transitioning and just needed to be made comfortable. Without knowledge we force liquids and foods into people who are transitioning in hopes of keeping them alive not realizing that it's difficult for them to swallow.

# THERE ARE NO BENEFITS IN OVERWORKING THE HIGH PERFORMERS

During the previous assignments I wanted to further my career, but time did not permit. I thought that I would become a registered nurse. As I continued to work as a certified nursing assistant, I realized how happy I made a lot of the patients and clients feel, and how much they tried to help me to help them.

After working with a cancer patient who wanted only myself to assist her, I decided to work assignments with multiple patients so as not to be confined in that manner. You see, she was given six months to live. After a year, the doctor said to her, "whatever you are doing keep it up." She was tube fed. She had dark circles around her eyes and lots of dark spots on her face when we first met. She was fed through her stomach, so I asked her, "you don't drink water," she replied, "no." I said to her, "you must drink water." She lived in a huge house with spiral stairs. When she realized the benefits of water, she had me travel up and down the stairs at least five, six, times a day to give her water, not to include the feeding and other details. She had a catheter, so she did not have to get up to urinate. She had a male friend who visited every day, he too had dark circles around his eyes. I needed a break so I asked if my daughter could relieve me for a day. She gave me a stern cold look and asked in a stern voice, "for how long?" I had already told her how long. I did not like that because I now had dark circles around my eyes. She and her male friend no longer had dark circles around their eyes. I relayed it to the necessary parties that I needed a day off besides my usual day off. They said that they were working on it. No one contacted me about relief. On my day off I asked them to get someone else. When I went back to pick up my check, they told me that I am to report it if someone is draining me. The patient threatened to close all accounts with her affiliates if someone did not get me back there. I did not question, nor did I reply. I took my check and left. I decided to work in a manner that would not confine me to one person.

A person's status should not be underestimated. I do not think that selfish people should absorb anyone's level of understanding and knowledge. When someone is giving their mental and physical strength, sometimes out of selfishness the receiver can unintentionally reject it.

# Being an Under Performer
# Can Be Disastrous

I was happy about the change that I made not to be confined to one person. I later learned as I practiced being a CNA, one on one or working to help multiple people, it is our choice to make a change, nevertheless I had become a pro in handling and caring for the patients that were assigned to me.

What I write is not to discredit but hopefully inspire that working together under any capacity is better than working against each other. My first experience in collaborating with a registered nurse and the way that nurse showed and helped me motivated me and made me proud to be a certified nurse assistant. I never saw him again, but he left an impact. I learned quickly, depending on where you are, that you either swam or you sank. I thought about my own mother when she was out there working as a PCA as a senior. I was not a senior when I started working as a PCA and a CNA, however she was the same age as some of her patients she was assigned to assist. I really learned a lot about aging or sick patients. I always treated each patient with respect and dignity. Those patients with dementia and Alzheimer weren't treated any differently because I know that there are moments where they see and understand. They may see and understand at a time they are feeling mistreated, so we get nothing from them in the way of help or support with care, mentally or physically. I did not find my job as a CNA suppressing or depressing. If I must work with a dementia or Alzheimer patient, I try to find a way to communicate. If we listen to them, we can get in where we fit in. If there were words that I could connect, oh it was on. We'd be talking and laughing or if the conversation were more serious, I would try to console such as saying things like "perhaps a cup of tea would help," if that person agreed then I would consult with the nurse to see if it's okay. Some thought that I was strange because there was no way a dementia or Alzheimer person can communicate in any form effectively. I heard one CNA say about me to the nurse, "she's not wrap too tight." Sometimes dementia and Alzheimer patients try to connect too because they sometimes mimic what we say or do. Having to assist or care for a combative dementia person can be disastrous so I try to be careful of my approach. I knock, I enter with a smile, I introduce myself. I do not touch their personal belongings without explaining a reason for doing so. I also address the reasons I am there, such as to help them get up and dressed for breakfast. I even tell them what's on the menu. Most times it works for me. Many were thinking but a few would say, "it is because of her appearance that she gets along with the clients, patients and residents." What I wear is not my character. If my disposition is distasteful, what I wear is distasteful also.

*I am not an analyst. I speak from my experiences.

When being trained to help with a paraplegic I wanted to by-pass the training section. Of course, it was not allowed, and the nurse was a professional to deny such a request. If we remind someone about the equipment Hoyer because we are trained and they are not interested, now I feel it's safer for me to work alone. When we feel that it is quicker to transport patients from bed to chair or from chair to bed without the proper thought or consideration for the good of all, it can be harmful. When I stepped out for work, I had already prepared myself mentally. Sometimes there were those who wanted to convince me that they were going to have a blessed night. I carried into prac-tice how to take my time when working on an assignment even though I was not given enough time. When the week was over and I was assigned to the paraplegic, I greeted him with a pleas-ant smile, "good morning," "how are you this morning?" After speaking I would say with a smile, "are we going to do this your way or my way?" That put a smile on his face. It's amazing what people can do when energy is transferred. He put every effort into turning his body to assist me. I got him bathe and dressed. I used the necessary equipment to get him up. His pleasant demeanor told me that he was satisfied with his level of care.

Moving along, I helped a lady and was warned by nurses to be careful, because she will beat the CNAs with her cane when approached. I was thinking why, would she do that and she's an old sickly lady? I can always move away from her. Nevertheless, I did heed the warning. I knocked on her door, greeted her, let her know that I am her nurse aide and if she should need anything I will happily assist her. She and others were appreciative. She was nice to me and always offered me a piece of candy. This nurse also wanted me to work according to the time she passed medication under the pretense that she wanted to help me. I noticed that she watched how I interacted with the patients. I noticed some disturbing things that could prove to be disastrous. She came to me to let me know that I was chosen to be interviewed by some people and the interviews were not something unusual, it's just that I was chosen at that time. She prompted me with lies as to what the questions would be and how to answer. As I answered questions asked by the interviewer, she said, "that's impossible." I explained why it was possible. If I had listened to that nurse, I would have been dumb founded because what she told me to say had nothing to do with what they wanted to know. I did not mention any names but let it be known that I felt uncomfortable working with a couple of nurses. Since nothing was done right away, I gave them a week's notice and kept a hawk eye watch for a week to give them time to replace me. As I was leaving that morning, she asks, "can you work tonight." I replied, no." I was there to be a help to and for the cause. Sometimes people do not have a clue what certified nursing assistants go through. I was asked the reason I left. I was also asked to return. I figured in time they will find out because such behavior is not limited to one person.

Some people apply for license for the wrong reasons and end up finding their career unproductive and boring, so they try to limit others.

I helped with a patient that was released from the hospital. She had brain surgery. Upon entering the new patient's room, I introduced myself but before I could go any further, she started crying, "I want to go home." I said to her "I understand, "stay here with us so that we can help you get better." She was crying again and said, "I want to go home." I said to her, "I am your nurse aide. I am going to do everything that I can to keep you comfortable. "Stay here with us, I promise before you know it, you will be cussing us out!" She laughed, but it was painful for her to laugh based on her facial expression. I explained to her how easy it was to communicate with me if she needed me before I returned. I tried to be professional as possible. As time progressed, she got better. I was amazed at what I could see, and the others could not. They did not know that she communicated with me on her first night. When I told the nurse that we communicated, she looked at me with slanted eyes, I smiled. She started swinging her leg off the bed, this put her at high fall risk, so her aids had to keep a watchful eye on her by sitting at her door. On my watch I told her, "I know what you are doing, "do not swing your leg off that bed because you may accidentally roll, even though the bed is close to the floor." She stayed in her bed. There was a nurse that was attentive to her patients, so I was happy when I got a chance to collaborate with her. I felt comfortable letting her know that she does things for attention. The nurse said, "she does not know what she is doing, and she cannot help herself." I had nothing to say. That nurse walked exceptionally light, so CNAs had to be careful slacking off. A couple of nights later I was walking in the direction of the patient's room, she saw me and swung her leg back on the bed. I turned around and the nurse was behind me. I asked her, "did you see that?" She replied, "yes, and I am shocked." Moving forward with the patient, I also found out that I had to be careful with my tone when speaking to her. She would sneak to the bathroom alone. I stopped saying that I am sorry to her. Those words made her cry some sorrowful tears. She told me that she was keeping her personal things in order. When she would lose her paperwork or forget where she put it, I told her to put it in her end table drawer. I told her those were her personal things, no one would touch them. I told her, if you are hiding things from us, you may be hiding them from yourself also so put them in your end table drawers. I will help you look for them later if I have time, if not tomorrow. I spotted a figure standing outside the door. A young lady came in and I could tell by her facial expression that she did not like what she heard. I got a phone call that evening asking me to explain what transpired that morning in her room. I started from the first day, explaining myself. I shared with him that she only wants an explanation on how to fix the situation. She goes into sorrowful tears when I whine about how sorry I am because she misplaced something. When we finished our conversation, he suggested that I close the door when in the room with a patient. That was the end of that, and I am being brief as some things said are confidential. Just as no one was there when we had our first interaction, no one was there when we had our last interaction. She said to me, "Barbara, thank you for everything, "I am going to miss you." She was going home.

While I am grateful for the outcome, whether we intend to be long term or short-term certified nursing assistants, we do our best so as not to feel inferior and unaccomplished.

# Performance Punishment

When helping with a combative woman, I must say that there was a CNA who had been helping her for a long time. She did ADLs with her and said to me if I need your help, I will ask for it. I found her to be genuine and I tried to help her in any way that I could and that included transporting the patient from bed to chair because she knew the techniques. Training with her was smooth and easy. I asked her, "why is it that she does not fight you?" She replied, "because I have been helping with her care for a long time and she knows that I am stronger." "I can transport her from bed to chair even though she is resisting." She asks me to get her up while she pretends to be busy doing something. She was hitting me when the CNA turned and said, "stop it." The patient saw that I could manage without assistance, so she calmed down. The CNA advised only make happy with her when all her care is done, otherwise she is going to try to beat you up. The others did not say pleasant things about the CNA when I first started, and it saddened me when I came to realize that she was a nice caring nurse aide. She was always nice to the patients and co-workers alike. She was moving to another county, so she trained me as the patient's new CNA. I missed her after she was gone because she was knowledgeable and pleasant to work with. We were helping with other patients, but that patient was combative. I came to realize that she fought with the CNAs when she couldn't do whatever she wanted to do and if she could do that, she wouldn't need help. She was transferred, so my help was no longer needed in that area. I was asked to work in an environment that was even worse. It was okay because I was going to create a peaceful environment there too.

I was met with sarcasm from a male certified nursing assistant. I don't know why or how he developed such an attitude towards me, so I tried to stay away from him. He had a sinister behavior (smiling around others) so trailing me was easy for him. The patients in my care were clean and happy, I made sure of that. Nurses wanted to collaborate with me because I did my job. I made life comfortable for the patients. Male CNAs or Female CNAs there should not be any partiality. We should work together for the benefit of the patients and be professional enough to decide what's best for patients and co-workers. That young man felt privileged being able to do as he pleased. He said to me, "you are not recognized." What he said did not phase me and that is because I know what I want to do, and I enjoy doing it. I chose CNA as a career so that is why I take it seriously and want to be a professional certified nursing assistant. I am not looking for any other career besides helping people. Those who did not have the mental and physical abilities to express themselves were left filthy and he was nowhere to be found whenever I relieved him. There were feces all over the room. For some reason I was not angry but extremely hurt. Because of the circumstances, I had no intentions of going anywhere, I knew that the situation would be fixed. Sometimes those who appear mentally incapable will surprise you. I had no idea that it would be fixed the same day. When I came to work that night, police cars were outside. When I got inside, I was told that he was brought up on serious charges. They took him away.

I worked helping the people for three months in that area. I was told when I came in one night that the person whom the assignment belonged to had returned. I needed that information confirmed. When helping with the patients I came to know their ADL needs. There was an HIV patient on that assignment. I liked the challenge of creating a peaceful and happy environment for myself and the patients. Whenever I sat down to relax, I earned it. I must admit that the HIV patient was slack when it came to doing anything for himself. I protected myself and cleaned him and his environment beautifully, three times before I sat down to have a serious talk with him. I was not afraid to speak my mind. He could have accepted or complained with distaste, it did not matter because my health is important to me. He was a young man. He changed drastically for the better and I was happy to assist him. After that somebody gave him all kinds of goodies. He had his little cupboard sat up, clothes hung up and in order. Those kinds of accomplishments made me feel good, so I was not going to stay around to be suppressed and depressed by continuing to do the job while someone else gets the credit for doing it. I would have been working in proximity so the first night I experienced what it was going to be like. I let it be known that I would not return that night. The lady lasted a month, so I am told. They contacted me but I was not interested.

Why am I writing about this? Some people lose their mental and physical strength because they do not know where to turn in such situations. They do not like what they have become, being a certified nursing assistant, so their behavior is projected onto co-workers and patients. How can we make patients happy if we are not happy? It is best if we work together as a team. Teamwork is working together to get things done in the proper way. Do not assume that a person who is doing their job properly is in some kind of desperate situation and is easy to manipulate. Do not ask someone to assist you with your work such as transporting a patient from bed to chair or from chair to bed when you do not have the strength to manage such weight thereby inflicting bodily injury on yourself, patients, and co-workers. Today there are all kinds of equipment for transporting and lifting patients. Patience is a virtue.

# Professionals Are to be Commended

I have worked many jobs. As I said, I usually do not like changing jobs but in this case, I thought about my mental and physical wellbeing. I found my career as a nursing assistant to be a fascinating experience. I found it to be a personally rewarding experience. I say this because many of the patients that I helped as a patient care aide or certified nursing assistant made great strides to assist with their care, making my job easier. It is amazing because as certified nursing assistants we interacted and helped many people with different professions from different walks of life.

I have met professional doctors and nurses. If they allowed me to remain in the examination room for whatever reason, I watched how they interacted with the patients. They did not let themselves be distracted by every question the patients asked while giving him or her their examinations. I did not let myself be distracted while doing things such as emptying a foley catheter because once that urine gets into your mouth or eyes, you cannot recall it. We thank those medical professionals who present themselves with authority showing, patients, clients, residents, that we are certified nurse assistants who were professionally trained by them rather than asking us to prohibit our talents. We commend you. Salute!

# PARTICIPATION IMPLIES TEAMWORK

I have worked with a lot of men. They were happy with my knowledge and techniques in the manner that I assisted them with their activities of daily living. I showed and was given a lot of respect, so I enjoyed helping them.

The men that I worked with were physically disabled. There were a few women but mostly men. I helped a man whose parachute did not open in time, so he fell and broke his body. He said some things that let me know that he was afraid of CNAs. He was afraid that us CNAs would hurt him even more. I'd rather the person be assigned two CNAs rather than asking, "can you help me?" Sometimes the CNA cannot help you when you want or need them so then the patient complains about an assistant. We both know that it is a part of our duty. I am sure someone would have helped because they had no choice. Those who worked that were family and friends happily helped each other. It is better for me to see the person's name beside mine, whose to collaborate with me. I wanted to be able to say I am ready, are you ready to do this together, rather than being uncomfortable approaching the person to ask for help. I knew that I had to do the job without pain or further injury to the patient. I took my time aligning his body on the side that was not injured. He felt more comfortable after that move. I was able to bathe, make his bed and dress him while in bed. Since he was not getting up that made the job easier. He was happy to share with anyone who would listen to what I had done for him. CNAs who learned what had transpired between him and I with his care wanted me to help them, but I was not able to help them in the manner that they wanted. Those who preferred to use their body weight to transport and lift patients were denied access to my body.

I tried to help with some CNAs, that's how I learned that some prefer that we use our bodies, thinking that this will get the job done quicker. If they did not understand the importance of using the necessary medical equipment for transporting and lifting patients, I did not take the chance of injuring myself. Our perseverance in doing our work in any other way except the techniques taught is not the same mindset. Body injury, mental and physical stress is inevitable. When a meeting was called because of my lack of teamwork, I was able to show and prove that it is not I, who is not practicing teamwork.

# MAKE ADL APPOINTMENTS

I helped a man who tried to do as much as possible for himself. One day he said to me, "no one is helping me but you." I explained to him that we are not all the same in age, knowledge, and maturity so we do not all give the same level of care. I told him not to be afraid to ask for help and accept the CNA's level of care if he or she meets all the necessary needs. After speaking with him I briefly explain some of the duties of the CNAs during the morning and evening shifts. I explained that time does not allow them to perform some of the duties that he is requesting. I told him that I work at night, if he wanted to get up and dressed in the morning, we could work out a time and agree on it so that his morning ADLs would be done before breakfast. Morning care was resolved, and it worked out for both of us.

# BEING GRUMPY DOES NOT MEAN THEY DO NOT WANT CARE

I was helping with a man on hospice with COPD. He was difficult to help because the CNAs were afraid of him. During the night there was not a lot to do for him except make sure that his head was elevated so that he could breathe better. I went into his room to get him bathed and dressed. When I entered the room, he started cursing, telling me to get the hell out. He was badly in need of a bath and shave. I told him that I was sent to help get him up for breakfast, that usually worked. I let him know that I was going to bathe, shave, and help him get dressed. He could be pivoted. He said, "if you touch me, "I am going to knock you out." I said to him, "look at me, "you are ill, at this time I am stronger than you." He said, 'I am not getting in that cold water." I learned how to give a bed bath that made a patient feel like he or she has had a full bath, so I told him, "I will bathe you in bed." I told him that he would not have to get out of bed to be bathed. I was able to bathe, shave and dress him while being told all the horrible things he was going to do to me, such as bury me in his back yard, then get the water hose, wet the dirt so that I could not breathe. I laughed so hard at the things that he was saying. Excuse my sense of humor (smile) but I was thinking, where is all this strength coming from in his voice. He doesn't look or sound like he's dying. He was a small man, so he was easy to transfer from bed to wheelchair. I could tell that he felt good. Upon my leaving he said, "I hope you're not coming back tomorrow." I Replied, "yes, so see you tonight." My co-workers were surprised at the quality of care that he received from me. He was awake and waiting for me. We went through the same routine the week that I visited with him. He enjoyed making me laugh so that he could continue to get that care. I was never intimidated by any of the patients. It's not that CNAs are afraid of him but by how things may be interpreted. A nurse heard him talking and she also heard me laughing. She reported that I was antagonizing him. Looking at his appearance and his demeanor. They asked me if everything was okay, I replied, "yes" and that was resolved. What prevented her from coming into the room? While they are to be protected from abuse, I think that she should have used her authority as a nurse to question her assistance rather than assume.

# WE SHOULD DO WHAT WE LIKE AND BE THE BEST AT IT

Upon being interviewed and hired for jobs I did not recognize or experience any inequity by interviewers or those in management.

I was in a situation at work where I was told that I would have to be moved away from the people that I was currently with. The only thing that I said to that remark is, "okay." When I worked the people that I helped would show their appreciation by thanking me, telling others about me, trying to give me something. When I was told that I was doing too much, that did not boost my spirit, nor did it break it. As I walked past, I heard one of the patients say with excitement, "there she is." He was told in a harsh tone, "stop it." They wanted me moved because I was getting too many complements, no problem, but when we must lie to justify the cause, we also must suffer the consequences. They bought the original supervisor in on it because these were newer supervisor and her assistant. I was brought up on some bogus charges and the person that they came to with the complaint, undoubtably found them to be liars because he suggests light duty and counseling. They told him he was wrong. When we stick together make sure we're not sticking up for what's wrong which is what they did. They asked me to write a reply explaining myself and we would discuss it the next day. They did not expect me to write what I wrote, and I am thinking that what I wrote did not make it to my file, but of course they will have to live with that if it did not. Because of my response the assistant supervisor had shifted her body into a position that should have been uncomfortable, exposing her as a liar. At the end of my response to them I wrote that this was also my resignation and gave my final date. I was told to write my resignation in a separate notice. Instead of two weeks, I wished that I had said a week. It was the longest two weeks. I did not know that I wanted to leave. I felt good knowing that I was on my way out. A day before I was due to leave, the supervisor asked, "would you like to stay?" I replied, no." Before my CNA career there were times when I felt mentally abused, so I would easily quit or retreat into misery and despair. In the past advocating for myself always ended up being a negative experience, so I tried even harder. There are certified nursing assistants who want to be nurses to escape such abuse. No matter what our title is, we still must be good people.

Here I am a certified nursing assistant who is certified to do activities of daily living to whoever it implies. I do patient care using my hands and realize that this must be done with care and professionalism. If we as certified nursing assistants get praises instead of complaints of distaste, we should not be penalized for it.

# I Did It for the Clients, Residents, and Patients

I have many years as a certified nursing assistant and would not have done it in this type of work with peace of mind and contentment if I had not been taught about myself and others and the proper handling of people. Certified nursing assistants work with a lot of people from diverse cultures. The Honorable Elijah Muhammad taught us to treat everybody how we would like to be treated. He said be good to everybody. I treat my co-workers and the people that I help, how I want to be treated.

I remember I walked into a man's room, he looked frustrated. He picked his pitcher up and started shaking it at me. I asked him, "you would like some water?" He continued to shake the pitcher. I looked around, saw canned drinks, and said, "ice" He shook his head as if he was relieved that I finally got it. I came back with the ice, picked up a can drink then asked in Spanish, "uno, dos, tres?" He replied, "dos." He smiled and looked happy until I said, "no hablo espanol muy bien." When I started tidying up and making him comfortable and we were making gestures to each other, that put a smile on his face. I learned those few words of Spanish when I was in junior high school. I wish that I had paid attention to my teacher.

Before                              After

Sometimes when I am helping a client, resident, or patient, I think about my own mother and father. I displayed knowledge and strength while doing my job. They awarded my high performance because they showed me that they appreciated what I did. I found myself moving from job to job, something that I normally did not like to do, moving and job hopping. I do not encourage CNAs or anyone else to job hop. That was my journey. I enjoyed working the nightshift. I liked working independently. When it came to being a certified nursing assistant, I did not think that we were allotted enough time to do an adequate job. Sometimes the people that we relieved did not have enough time to do an adequate job either. Some of us as little miracle workers made it happen though. What does not count is when we do not do our job at all. I did not sleep at night, so I was busy taking care of what needed to be done. When others have gotten their rest, clients, residents, patients, and co-workers during the night, I have no problem with that. A constant we must take on patients in the wee hours because someone is leaving, doesn't work for me. I was working during the night so to avoid being overworked, so that those who were under performers could be rewarded was detrimental to my well-being. Struggling to manage responsibilities that others left at the wrong time can be stressful. In haste we're doing this,

When we should be doing this?

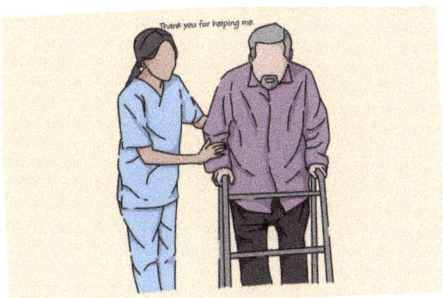

Less chances of anybody getting hurt.

# LIFE BECOMES EASIER WHEN WE DO THE RIGHT THING

It is really something when you don't want people that you work with to know how resourceful you can be, but I had no choice. Covid was spreading. A nurse tested positive, so the area was off limits. No one wanted it, so I took it. As I mentioned before I liked working independently. Co-workers were congregating, enjoying their morning before they got started. I geared up and willed myself to make sure that everything went smoothly by getting breakfast and other activities of daily living done in a timely manner. The nurse helped me with breakfast. He managed his business, and I managed mine. While working as a certified nursing assistant, I am gratefully and amazingly blessed. After breakfast was accomplished, I was asked by a nurse who was congregating with the others and now eating breakfast, to help other CNAs with breakfast. I reminded her of the protocol regarding covid and suggested that she help since she had to go into that area anyway. Somehow it seems like that kind of critical thinking isn't permitted by a nursing assistant.

On another note, I know a few certified nursing assistants who have tried for years to become a nurse. In all that you encounter there is a negative side and there is a positive side. Think about it and take the positive side.

I know that as we age and get older, especially in our senior years, we wonder about help and support. I say we must try to take care of our health so that we can remain strong mentally and physically. The people that I worked with did not know my age, so I listened to some of their complaints as to why they wanted to be a nurse. Remember I said that I met some good doctors and nurses who explained and trained well. I remember one of my earlier jobs when I first got started as a certified nursing assistant. I was helping this lady who had elephantiasis legs, huge, crusty, and hard. I bathed and applied medication to her legs every day. They were stiff. I tried to gently exercise them. One day a doctor visited and complemented her about her legs then she turned to me and began telling me other things to do. That lady put a horrible looking frown on her face and said to the doctor, "you don't have to explain anything to her, she "ain't nobody." The doctor asked me to come into the kitchen then said, "she is sick, she doesn't mean any harm." I smiled and said, "it's okay." The sister that

I originally started with went on vacation for a week. Another sister came to be with the mom while she was away. Her spirit was warm and a kind person who did not seem to have a clue. I had planned not to return but I did not want to leave her alone, so I stayed until that week was up. I did not come back on the date that her sister was supposed to return home. I played my phone messages and heard her mom on the phone, yelling, "call her again, you are not trying to call her." The pay was a few dollars, I was trying to help her, but she was unappreciative. I did not feel discouraged by her words. The doctor approved that level of care and shared information that I could use in the future.

Another time, one certified nurse assistant that I was working with was studying to be a nurse. She told one of the other nurses that she was going to get me fired once she became a nurse. I was told that she was fired for saying that. Remember the original supervisor who did not stick up for me but against me with the supervisor and assistant on the other job. She ended up working on the same job and said to the people one morning "Barbara is awesome." I was not impressed. I wondered why she left such a high paying job. If you want to be a nurse, be a nurse because you want to help people. If you want to be a nursing assistant, be a nursing assistant because you want to help people. It's not always easy but the outcome is better if we do the right thing.

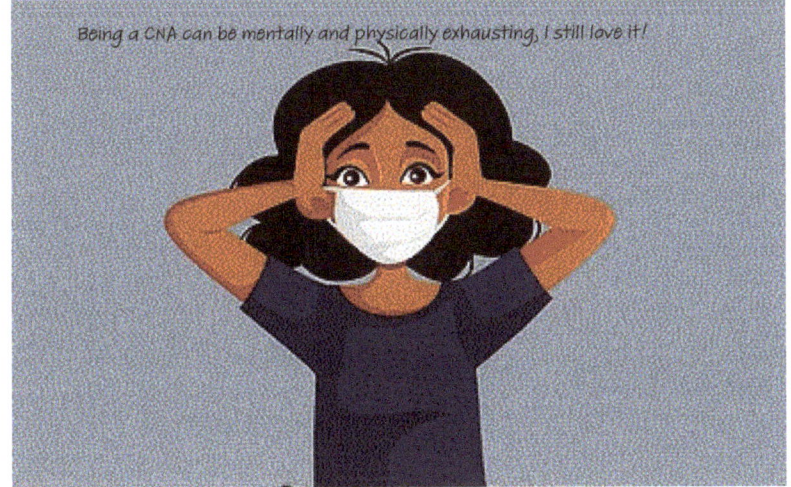

# WHY BE A CERTIFIED NURSING ASSISTANT

Have you ever asked yourself, why do I want to be a certified nursing assistant? I thought to myself we cannot all be registered nurses, licensed practical nurses, and certified nursing assistants. There needs to be a balance. During my earlier years as a certified nursing assistant, I gave up wanting to be a CNA twice. I missed meeting and helping the people. I decided to continue working as a CNA. As I said earlier in my writing that I thought that I wanted to be a registered nurse but seeing how happy I made so many people feel, I changed my mind. This is where I learned that we must be happy with the career that we have chosen. If we are not happy doing what we like, how can we transfer that happiness to others? I am taught if we are given a job do not hide to avoid work. I am also taught that if you can give a little extra do the little extra work. Some people mistake doing a little extra as foolish, weak, desperate, or being used. Most could not conceive or view that as striving for perfection. Things may not have turned out perfectly, but it always turned out in a goodly manner. To see people feeling rejuvenated and smiling because of the level of care or services that we as certified nursing assistants have rendered is a personally rewarding feeling to the caregiver. Some of them take pride in their appearance so I delighted in telling them how handsome or beautiful they looked on that day.

# IT'S A BEAUTIFUL GIFT TO HELP ONE PURSUE THEIR GOAL TOWARDS WELLNESS

It's really something when the mind works but the body doesn't work as well, or the body works, and the mind doesn't work as well. Either way when we start to lose ourselves to illnesses, it can be a scary situation, so we need loving and caring people to assist us. Saying unwholesome things about the nursing assistants does not boost the ego. Saying such things as, I wouldn't want that type of job because it is a butt wiping job and I am paraphrasing, can make a potential CNA change his or her mind. If we keep on living, we may one day need someone to wipe our butt. Hospitals, assistant living, nursing homes, group homes, homecare are some of the businesses that require a certified nursing assistant. There is more to being a certified nursing assistant than cleaning body waste or feces. There are seniors that are not in assistance living or nursing homes. Some live independently and may want or need assistance. They can give instructions as to their wants and needs. For instance, a ninety-four-year-old living alone under the guidance of their loved ones, who needs assistance with meal preps and medication reminder. A senior who may need assistance with food shopping and laundry or appointments. Sometimes they are not asking for a lot, but they want someone who is going to help brighten their day so that they can rise, shine, and give compliments for a beautiful day.

www.ingramcontent.com/pod-product-compliance
Lightning Source LLC
Chambersburg PA
CBHW051243120626
46547CB00014B/1780